BAKE YOUR OWN
CUPCAKES

BY MARI BOLTE

PEBBLE
a capstone imprint

Published by Pebble, an imprint of Capstone
1710 Roe Crest Drive, North Mankato, Minnesota 56003
capstonepub.com

Copyright © 2026 by Capstone. All rights reserved. No part of this publication may be reproduced in whole or in part, or stored in a retrieval system, or transmitted in any form or by any means, electronic, mechanical, photocopying, recording, or otherwise, without written permission of the publisher.

Library of Congress Cataloging-in-Publication Data
Names: Bolte, Mari, author.
Title: Bake your own cupcakes / by Mari Bolte.
Description: North Mankato, Minnesota : Pebble, an imprint of Capstone, [2026] | Series: Pebble maker baking | Audience: Ages 5–8 | Audience: Grades 2–3 | Summary: "It's a party with this festive dessert! Early and emergent readers can bake their own batch of sprinkle cupcakes topped with colorful vanilla frosting. Step-by-step instructions plus clear photos guide elementary children through this simple and sweet recipe that they (with a little adult assistance) can make themselves—and then enjoy!"— Provided by publisher.
Identifiers: LCCN 2024052315 (print) | LCCN 2024052316 (ebook) | ISBN 9798875224386 (hardcover) | ISBN 9798875224331 (paperback) | ISBN 9798875224348 (pdf) | ISBN 9798875224355 (epub) | ISBN 9798875224362 (kindle edition)
Subjects: LCSH: Cupcakes—Juvenile literature. | LCGFT: Cookbooks.
Classification: LCC TX771 .B653 2026 (print) | LCC TX771 (ebook) | DDC 641.86/53—dc23/eng/20241205
LC record available at https://lccn.loc.gov/2024052315
LC ebook record available at https://lccn.loc.gov/2024052316

Editorial Credits
Editor: Abby Cich; Designer: Heidi Thompson; Media Researcher: Jo Miller; Production Specialist: Tori Abraham

Image Credits
Capstone: Karon Dubke, front and back cover, 1, 9, 11–20, 21 (cupcake); Shutterstock: 5 second Studio, 5, Iris Sokolovskaya, 21 (loose sprinkles), PeopleImages.com - Yuri A, 7, yvonnestewarthenderson, 23

The publisher and the author shall not be liable for any damages allegedly arising from the information in this book, and they specifically disclaim any liability from the use or application of any of the contents of this book.

Any additional websites and resources referenced in this book are not maintained, authorized, or sponsored by Capstone. All product and company names are trademarks™ or registered® trademarks of their respective holders.

Printed and bound in China. 6274

TABLE OF CONTENTS

Cute Cakes 4

Kitchen Tips 6

What You Need 8

What You Do 10

Take It Further 22

Glossary 24

About the Author 24

Words in **BOLD** are in the glossary.

CUTE CAKES

People have been enjoying cupcakes for hundreds of years. They can be many flavors. Frosting and toppings can give them a fun look. Cupcakes are often used to celebrate special events.

But you don't need a special reason to enjoy some. Bake your own cupcakes!

KITCHEN TIPS

Stay safe and have fun with these tips.

- Have an adult helper nearby. Ask them to help with hot or sharp things.

- Read the recipe before you start. Get all your **ingredients** and tools.

- Wash your hands before you begin.

- Help clean up when you are done!

WHAT YOU NEED

INGREDIENTS FOR THE CUPCAKES

- 1/2 cup (113 grams) unsalted butter, room temperature

- 3/4 cup (148 g) white sugar

- 2 eggs, room temperature

- 1 teaspoon (5 milliliters) vanilla **extract**

- 1 1/2 cups (180 g) flour

- 1/2 cup (118 mL) milk, room temperature

- 1 1/2 teaspoons (6 g) baking powder

- 1/2 teaspoon (3 g) salt

- 1/4 cup (48 g) sprinkles

INGREDIENTS FOR THE FROSTING

- 1/2 cup (113 g) unsalted butter, room temperature
- 2 cups (227 g) powdered sugar
- 1 teaspoon (5 mL) vanilla extract
- pinch of salt
- 2 tablespoons (10 mL) milk
- gel food coloring in your favorite color

TOOLS

- **cupcake liners**
- 12-cup muffin pan
- measuring cups and spoons
- mixing bowl and spoon
- **hand mixer**
- cooling rack
- butter knife

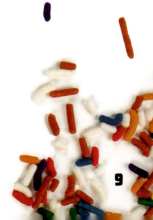

WHAT YOU DO

STEP 1

Put a cupcake liner in each cup of the muffin pan. Ask an adult to **preheat** the oven to 350°F (175°C).

STEP 2

Put the butter and sugar into the mixing bowl. Use the hand mixer to **beat** for 3 minutes or so. Go until the **mixture** is light and fluffy.

Crack the eggs into the bowl. Pick out any shell with a spoon. Add the vanilla extract. Beat for 3 minutes more.

STEP 3

Add a 1/2 cup (60 g) of the flour to the bowl. Stir it in with the mixing spoon. Pour in the milk. Stir just until it is mixed in. Then add the other 1 cup (120 g) of flour. Put in the baking powder, salt, and sprinkles too. Gently stir till there are no dry spots.

STEP 4

Grab a 1/4 measuring cup. Use it to fill all the liners evenly with **batter**.

Ask the adult to bake the cupcakes for 20 to 25 minutes. Are the cakes golden brown? They are done! With the adult's help, take them out of the pan. Set them on the cooling rack. Cool at least 1 hour.

STEP 5

Frosting time! Wash the hand mixer beaters. Wash the bowl too, or take out a new one. Put the butter in the bowl. Beat till it is fluffy. Add 1/2 cup (57 g) of powdered sugar. Beat again. Repeat till all the sugar is mixed in.

Add the vanilla extract, salt, and milk. Beat for 3 to 4 minutes. Put in a bit of food coloring. Stir until the frosting is one color.

STEP 6

Use a butter knife to put frosting on the cupcakes. Add sprinkles on top. Enjoy your treats! Store extras in a dish with a lid. Eat them in 2 to 4 days.

TAKE IT FURTHER

Want even more color? Add some food coloring to the batter too.

Try a new topping! Instead of sprinkles, use mini chocolate chips. Fruit or candy also works great.

Make chocolate frosting! Add 2 tablespoons (10 g) of cocoa powder to the powdered sugar.

GLOSSARY

batter (BAT-uhr)—a wet mixture that can be poured, usually made of at least flour and a liquid

beat (BEET)—to mix food by stirring in a fast circular motion

cupcake liner (KUP-keyk LAHY-ner)—a cup-shaped piece of paper or foil used to hold batter in a muffin pan; liners keep food from sticking to the pan

extract (EK-strakt)—a liquid used for flavoring food

hand mixer (HAND MIKS-er)—a handheld electric tool with two beaters that can turn quickly

ingredient (in-GREE-dee-uhnt)—a food that is put with other foods to make a recipe

mixture (MIKS-cher)—two or more ingredients that have been mixed together

preheat (PREE-heet)—to heat an oven to a certain temperature before baking

ABOUT THE AUTHOR

Mari Bolte has been baking—and writing books about baking—since the beginning of time. (Well, it feels like that, anyway.) These days, she squeezes in loaves of no-knead bread and trays of sweet treats in between writing projects.